Ludw
Beethoven

The Biography of a Genius Composer and his Famous Moonlight Sonata Revealed

By United Library

https://campsite.bio/unitedlibrary

Table of Contents

Disclaimer

This biography book is a work of nonfiction based on the public life of a famous person. The author has used publicly available information to create this work. While the author has thoroughly researched the subject and attempted to depict it accurately, it is not meant to be an exhaustive study of the subject. The views expressed in this book are those of the author alone and do not necessarily reflect those of any organization associated with the subject. This book should not be taken as an endorsement, legal advice, or any other form of professional advice. This book was written for entertainment purposes only.

Introduction

Ludwig van Beethoven was a German composer and pianist who is widely considered one of the greatest composers of all time. In his early years, he used the works of Joseph Haydn and Wolfgang Amadeus Mozart as inspiration for his own compositions. He had immense influence in transitioning from the Classical period to the Romantic era in classical music. His career can be divided into three periods: early (1770-1802), middle (1802-1812) and late (1812- 1827).

Over this course of his life, he wrote some of the most influential symphonies, chamber pieces, sonatas and operas known to man - including Fidelio, Missa Solemnis and Symphony No. 9. Despite gradually becoming deaf during this period, his genius persisted undeterred until he passed away at age 56 due to illness.

Beethoven's compositions have become an important part of modern day classical music repertoire that continues to inspire generations everywhere even today!

Ludwig van Beethoven

Ludwig van Beethoven was a German composer, pianist and conductor, born in Bonn on December 15 or 16, 1770 and died in Vienna on March 26, 1827 at the age of 56.

The last great representative of Viennese classicism (after Gluck, Haydn and Mozart), Beethoven paved the way for the evolution of Romanticism in music and influenced Western music for a large part of the XIXe century. Unclassifiable ("You give me the impression of a man with many heads, many hearts, many souls," said Haydn to him around 1793), his art was expressed through different musical genres, and although his symphonic music is the main source of his popularity, he also had a considerable impact in piano writing and chamber music.

Overcoming by dint of will the trials of a life marked by deafness which struck him at the age of 27, celebrating in his music the triumph of heroism and joy when destiny imposed isolation and misery, he was rewarded *post mortem* by this statement by Romain Rolland: "He is much more than the first of the musicians. He is the most heroic force of modern art". As an expression of an unshakeable faith in man and of a voluntary optimism, as an affirmation of a free and independent artist,

Beethoven's work made him one of the most important figures in the history of music.

Biography

Origins and childhood

Ludwig van Beethoven was born in Bonn, Rhineland, on December 15 or 16, 1770, into a modest family that had carried on a musical tradition for at least two generations.

His paternal grandfather, Ludwig van Beethoven the Elder (1712-1773), was descended from a commoner Flemish family from Mechelen (the preposition *van*, "de," in Dutch surnames is not a noble particle, unlike the German *von*, equivalent to the French "de"). A respected man and good musician, he moved to Bonn in 1732 and became Kapellmeister to the Elector of Cologne, Clement Augustus of Bavaria.

His father, Johann van Beethoven (1740-1792), was a musician and tenor at the Elector's Court. A mediocre man, brutal and alcoholic, he raised his children with the greatest rigor. His mother, Maria-Magdalena van Beethoven, born Keverich (1746-1787), is the daughter of a cook of the Archbishop-Elector of Trier. Depicted as self-effacing, gentle and depressive, she was loved by her children. Ludwig is the second of seven children, of whom only three reach adulthood: himself, Kaspar-Karl (1774-1815) and Johann (1776-1848).

It did not take long for Johann van Beethoven, the father, to detect his son's musical gift and to realize the exceptional benefits he could draw from it. Thinking of the child Wolfgang Amadeus Mozart, who had been performed in concerts all over Europe fifteen years earlier, he undertook Ludwig's musical education as early as 1775 and, in view of his exceptional abilities, tried in 1778 to introduce him to the piano throughout the Rhineland, from Bonn to Cologne. But where Leopold Mozart had shown a subtle pedagogy with his son, Johann van Beethoven seems only capable of authoritarianism and brutality, and this experience remains unsuccessful, with the exception of a tour in the Netherlands in 1781 where the young Beethoven was appreciated, but still without the financial returns that his father hoped for.

There is no picture of Beethoven's parents, Bettina Mosler having demonstrated that the two portraits published at the beginning of the twentieth century as postcards by the Beethoven-Haus in Bonn were not those of his parents.

Ludwig left school at the end of primary school at the age of 11. His general education is due in large part to the kindness of the von Breuning family (where he now spends most of his days and sometimes some nights) and to his friendship with the physician Franz-Gerhard Wegeler, people to whom he was attached all his life. The young Ludwig became a pupil of Christian Gottlob Neefe (piano, organ, composition) who gave him a taste for polyphony by introducing him to Bach's *Well-Tempered Clavier.* Between 1782 and 1783, he composed for the piano the *9 variations on a march by Dressler* and the three *Sonatines* known as "à l'Électeur" which symbolically mark the beginning of his musical production. As a child, his dark complexion earned him the nickname of "l'Espagnol": this melanoderma led to the suspicion of hemochromatosis, the cause of his chronic cirrhosis, which developed from 1821 and was to be the cause of his death.

Waldstein's patronage and Haydn's encounter

At the time when his father was drinking more and more and his mother was suffering from tuberculosis, Beethoven became, at the age of 14 in 1784, assistant organist at the court of the new elector Max-Franz, who became his protector. Having become the breadwinner of the family, in addition to this position, he was obliged to give more piano lessons.

Beethoven was noticed by Count Ferdinand von Waldstein, whose role was decisive for the young musician. He took Beethoven to Vienna for the first time in April 1787, during which time he had a furtive meeting with Wolfgang Amadeus Mozart: "At Mozart's request, Beethoven played him something that Mozart, taking it for a ceremonial piece learned by heart, approved of rather coldly. Beethoven, having noticed this, asked him to give him a theme on which to improvise, and, as he was in the habit of playing admirably when excited, inspired moreover by the presence of the master for whom he professed such great respect, he played in such a way that Mozart, slipping into the adjoining room where some of his friends were standing, said to them briskly: "*Pay attention to this one, he will be the talk of the world*.

In July 1787, Ludwig's mother dies, which plunges him into despair. Beethoven's family consists of his brothers Kaspar Karl (13 years old) and Nicolas (11 years old), as well as his sister Maria Margarita who dies in November, while his father sinks into alcoholism and poverty. He will be retired in 1789.

In May 1789, Beethoven - aware of his cultural deficiencies - enrolled at the University of Bonn to take courses in German literature. His professor Euloge Schneider was enthusiastic about the French Revolution and spoke about it ardently to his students. In 1791, during a trip of the Elector Max-Franz to the castle of Mergentheim, Beethoven meets the pianist and composer Johann Franz Xaver Sterkel, who deeply influences Beethoven's piano playing and develops his taste for this instrument.

In July 1792, Count Waldstein introduced the young Ludwig to Joseph Haydn who, on his way back from a tour in England, had stopped in Bonn. Impressed by the reading of a cantata composed by Beethoven (the one *on the death of Joseph II* or the one *on the advent of Leopold II*) and while being lucid on the deficiencies of his education, Haydn invites him to study in Vienna under his direction. Aware of the opportunity that the teaching of a musician of Haydn's reputation represented in Vienna, and almost deprived of his family ties in Bonn, Beethoven accepted. On November 2, 1792, he left the banks of the Rhine, never to return, taking with him this recommendation from Waldstein: "Dear Beethoven, you are going to Vienna to fulfill a wish that has long been expressed: the genius of Mozart is still in mourning and mourns the death of his disciple. In the inexhaustible Haydn he finds a refuge, but not an occupation; through him he still wishes to unite with someone. By unceasing application, receive from Haydn's hands the spirit of Mozart."

Beethoven's father died in December of 1792, and there was no longer any connection between Beethoven and Bonn.

1792-1802: from Vienna to Heiligenstadt

Early Viennese years

[e]At the end of the 18th century, Vienna was the capital of Western music and represented the best chance for a musician to succeed. Twenty-two years old when he arrived, Beethoven had already composed a great deal, but hardly anything of importance. Although he arrived in Vienna less than a year after Mozart's death, the myth of the "passing of the torch" between the two artists is unfounded: still very far from his artistic maturity, it is not as a composer but as a virtuoso pianist that Beethoven forges his reputation in Vienna.

As for Haydn's teaching, as prestigious as it was, it proved to be disappointing in many ways. On the one hand, Beethoven quickly realized that his teacher was jealous of him and denied his influence; on the other hand, Haydn was quick to become irritated by the indiscipline and musical audacity of his student, whom he called the "Great Mogul. In spite of Haydn's profound and lasting influence on Beethoven's work, and a mutual esteem often recalled by the latter, the "father of the symphony" never had with Beethoven the relationship of deep friendship that he had had with Mozart and which had been at the origin of such a fertile emulation.

"You have a lot of talent and you will acquire even more, enormously more. You have an inexhaustible abundance of inspiration, you will have thoughts that no one has yet had, you will never sacrifice your thought to a tyrannical rule, but you will sacrifice the rules to your fancies; for you make me feel like a man who has many heads, many hearts, many souls."

- Haydn, around 1793.

In January 1794, after Haydn's new departure for London, Beethoven continued episodic studies until the beginning of 1795 with various other teachers, including the composer Johann Schenk, with whom he became friends, and two other witnesses of the Mozart era: Johann Georg Albrechtsberger and Antonio Salieri. After his apprenticeship, Beethoven settled permanently in the Austrian capital. His talents as a pianist and his gifts as an improviser made him known and appreciated by the music-loving personalities of the Viennese aristocracy, whose names are still attached to the dedications of several of his masterpieces: Baron Nikolaus Zmeskall, Prince Carl Lichnowsky, Count Andrei Razoumovski, Prince Joseph Franz von Lobkowitz, and later Archduke Rudolph of Austria, to name but a few.

After publishing his first three *Trios for piano, violin and cello* under the number Opus 1, and then his first *Piano Sonatas*, Beethoven gave his first public concert on March 29, 1795 for the premiere of his *Piano Concerto No.° 2* (which was in fact composed first, at the time in Bonn).

The first virtuoso of Vienna and first masterpieces (The Great Master)

1796. Beethoven undertook a concert tour that took him from Vienna to Berlin, passing through Dresden, Leipzig, Nuremberg and Prague. If the public praised his virtuosity and his inspiration at the piano, his ardor earned him the skepticism of the most conservative critics. A music critic of the *Journal patriotique des Etats impériaux et royaux* reported in October 1796: "He captures our ears, not our hearts; that is why he will never be a Mozart for us.

The reading of the Greek classics, Shakespeare and the leaders of the *Sturm und Drang* movement, Goethe and Schiller, had a lasting influence on the temperament of the musician, who also embraced the democratic ideals of the Enlightenment and the French Revolution, which were spreading throughout Europe: In 1798, Beethoven assiduously frequented the French embassy in Vienna where he met Bernadotte and the violinist Rodolphe Kreutzer to whom he dedicated, in 1803, the *Sonata for violin n° 9* which bears his name.

While his creative activity intensifies (composition of the *Sonatas for piano* n° 5 to n° 7, of the first *Sonatas for violin and piano*), the composer participates until around 1800 in musical jousts which Viennese society loves and which consecrate him as the greatest virtuoso of Vienna to the detriment of famous pianists like Clementi, Cramer, Gelinek, Hummel and Steibelt.

The end of the 1790s was also the time of the first masterpieces, which are embodied in the *Romance for violin and orchestra no.° 2* (1798), the *Piano Concerto no.° 1* (1798), the first six *String Quartets* (1798-1800), the *Septet* for strings and winds (1799-1800), and in the two works that most clearly assert the musician's nascent character: the *Grande Sonate pathétique* (1798-1799) and the *First Symphony* (1800). Although the influence of Haydn's later symphonies is apparent, the latter is already imbued with a Beethovenian character (especially in the third movement scherzo). The *First Concerto* and the *First Symphony* were performed with great success on April 2, 1800, the date of Beethoven's first academy (a concert that the musician devoted entirely to his works).

Comforted by the income he received from his patrons, Beethoven, whose reputation was growing beyond the borders of Austria, seemed at this time of his life to be destined for a glorious and comfortable career as a composer and performer.

"His improvisation could not have been more brilliant and astonishing; in whatever society he found himself, he succeeded in producing such an impression on each of his listeners that it frequently happened that their eyes became wet with tears, and many burst into tears. There was something wonderful in his expression, apart from the beauty and originality of his ideas and the ingenious way in which he rendered them."

- Carl Czerny

The turn of the century

The year 1802 marked the first major turning point in the composer's life. Suffering from tinnitus, he began in 1796 to become aware of a deafness that would irreparably progress until it became total before 1820. Forcing himself into isolation for fear of having to face this terrible truth in public, Beethoven earned a reputation as a misanthrope, from which he would suffer in silence until the end of his life. Aware that his infirmity would sooner or later prevent him from performing as a pianist and perhaps from composing, he considered suicide for a moment, and then expressed both his sadness and his faith in his art in a letter that has come down to us as the "Testament of Heiligenstadt", which was never sent and only found after his death:

Beethoven, October 6, 1802." O you men who think that I am a hateful, obstinate, misanthropic being, or who make me seem so, how unjust you are! You do not know the secret reason for what appears to you to be so. [...] Consider that for six years I have been struck by a terrible illness, which incompetent doctors have aggravated. Year after year, disappointed by the hope of an improvement, [...] I had to isolate myself early, to live alone, far from the world. [...] If you ever read this, then think that you have not been fair to me, and that the unfortunate one consoles himself by finding someone who resembles him and who, in spite of all the obstacles of Nature, has nevertheless done everything to be admitted to the rank of artists and men of value."

Fortunately, his creative vitality did not suffer. After the composition of the tender *Violin Sonata n° 5* called *Spring* (*Frühlings*, 1800) and the *Piano Sonata n° 14* called *Moonlight* (1801), it is in this period of moral crisis that he composed the joyful and unknown *Second Symphony* (1801-1802) and the darker *Piano Concerto n° 3* (1800-1802) in which the characteristic personality of the composer, in the key of C minor, clearly appears. These two works were very favorably received on April 5, 1803, but for Beethoven a page was turned. From then on, his career took a turn.

"I am not very satisfied with my work so far. Starting today, I want to blaze a new trail."

- Beethoven in Krumpholz, in 1802.

Deprived of the possibility of expressing all his talent and earning a living as a performer, he devoted himself to composition with great strength of character. At the end of the crisis of 1802, the triumphant heroism of the *Third Symphony,* known as the "*Eroica*", is announced.

1802-1812: The *Heroic* Period

The *Third Symphony*, *"Eroica,"* marks a milestone in Beethoven's work, not only because of its expressive power and hitherto unprecedented length, but also because it inaugurates a series of brilliant works, remarkable in their duration and energy, characteristic of Beethoven's middle period style, known as the "Eroica style. The composer initially intended to dedicate this symphony to General Napoleon Bonaparte, First Consul of the French Republic, in whom he saw the savior of the ideals of the Revolution. But upon learning of the proclamation of the French Empire (May 1804), he went into a rage and fiercely erased the dedication, replacing the title *Buonaparte* with the phrase *"Grande symphonie*

Héroïque pour célébrer le souvenir d'un grand homme". The genesis of the symphony stretches from 1802 to 1804 and the public premiere, on April 7, 1805, unleashes passions, with almost everyone judging it to be much too long. Beethoven did not care, declaring that this symphony would be found very short when he had composed one lasting more than an hour, and considering - until the composition of the *Ninth* - the *Eroica* as the best of his symphonies.

In 1804, the piano *Sonata n° 21,* dedicated to Count Waldstein, whose name it bears, strikes the performers with its great virtuosity and the abilities it demands of the instrument. From a similar mold comes the dark and grandiose *Piano Sonata no.° 23* called *Appassionata* (1805), which follows shortly after the *Triple Concerto* for piano, violin, cello and orchestra (1804). In July 1805, the composer met Luigi Cherubini, for whom he did not hide his admiration.

At the age of thirty-five, Beethoven tackled the genre in which Mozart had been most successful: opera. In 1801, he had been enthusiastic about the libretto *Leonore or Conjugal Love* by Jean-Nicolas Bouilly, and the opera *Fidelio*, which originally bore the title of his heroine *Leonore*, was sketched out in 1803. But the work gave its author unexpected difficulties. Poorly received at the beginning (only three performances in 1805), Beethoven considered himself the victim of a cabal. *Fidelio* underwent no less than three reworkings (1805, 1806 and 1814), and it was not until the last one that the opera was finally given a reception worthy of it. Although he had composed a major piece of the operatic repertoire, this experience was bitter for the composer and he never returned to this genre, even though he studied several other projects, including a *Macbeth* inspired by Shakespeare's work and, above all, a *Faust* after Goethe, at the end of his life.

Asserted independence

After 1805, despite the resounding failure of *Fidelio*, Beethoven's situation became favorable again. In full possession of his creative vitality, he seems to have come to terms with his failing hearing and to have found, for a time at least, a satisfactory social life. If the failure of an intimate relationship with Josephine von Brunsvik (de) is a new sentimental disillusionment for the musician, the years 1806 to 1808 are the most fertile of his creative life: the year 1806 alone sees the composition of the *Piano Concerto n° 4*, of the three *String Quartets n° 7, n° 8 and n° 9* dedicated to the Count Andreï Razoumovski, of the *Fourth Symphony* and of the *Violin Concerto*. In the autumn of this year, Beethoven accompanies his patron, Prince Carl Lichnowsky, to his castle in Silesia, which has been occupied by Napoleon's army since Austerlitz, and during this stay he makes the most striking demonstration of his will to be independent. Lichnowsky had threatened to arrest Beethoven if he persisted in refusing to play the piano for French officers stationed in his castle. The composer left his host after a violent quarrel and sent him the following bill:

"Prince, what you are, you are by chance of birth. What I am, I am by myself.
There have been princes and there will be thousands more. There is only one Beethoven.

- Beethoven to Lichnowsky, October 1806.

Although he got into trouble by losing the income of his main patron, Beethoven managed to assert himself as an independent artist and to symbolically free himself from aristocratic patronage. From then on, the heroic style could reach its paroxysm. Following up on his wish to "seize fate by the throat," expressed to Wegeler in November 1801, Beethoven began work on the *Fifth Symphony*. Through his famous rhythmic motif of four notes preceded by a silence, which is exposed from the first bar and which radiates throughout the work, the musician intends to express man's struggle with his destiny, and his final triumph. The *Coriolan* Overture, with which it shares the key of C minor, dates from the same period. Composed at the same time as the *Fifth*, the *Pastoral Symphony* seems all the more contrasted.

Described by Michel Lecompte as "the most serene, the most relaxed, the most melodic of the nine symphonies" and at the same time the most atypical, it is the homage to nature of a composer deeply in love with the countryside, in which he has always found the calm and serenity conducive to his inspiration. A true harbinger of Romanticism in music, the *Pastoral is* subtitled by Beethoven: "Expression of feeling rather than painting" and each of its movements bears a descriptive indication: the program symphony was born.

The concert given by Beethoven on December 22, 1808 is without a doubt one of the greatest "academies" in history, along with that of May 7, 1824. The *Fifth Symphony*, the *Pastoral Symphony*, the *Piano Concerto n° 4*, the *Choral Fantasy* for piano and orchestra and two hymns from the *Mass in C major* composed for Prince Esterházy in 1807 were played in the first audition. This was Beethoven's last appearance as a soloist. Unable to obtain an official position in Vienna, he had decided to leave the city and wanted to show it the extent of what it was losing. Following this concert, patrons provided him with an annuity that allowed him to remain in the capital. After Haydn's death in May 1809, although he still had some determined opponents, there were hardly anyone left to dispute Beethoven's place in the musical pantheon.

Artistic maturity

In 1808, Beethoven was offered the position of Kapellmeister at the Court of Kassel by Jerome Bonaparte, then King of Westphalia. It seems that, for a moment, the composer thought of accepting this prestigious position which, if it challenged his dearly defended independence, would have assured him a comfortable social situation. It was then that the Viennese aristocracy had a patriotic awakening (1809). Refusing to let their national musician leave, Archduke Rudolph, Prince Kinsky and Prince Lobkowitz joined forces to ensure Beethoven, if he remained in Vienna, a life annuity of 4,000 florins per year, a considerable sum for the time. Beethoven accepts, seeing his hope of being definitively free of need succeed, but the resumption of the war between Austria and France in the spring of 1809 puts everything in question. The imperial family was forced to leave occupied Vienna, the serious economic crisis that took hold of Austria after Wagram and the treaty of Schönbrunn imposed by Napoleon ruined the aristocracy and caused the devaluation of the Austrian currency. Beethoven had difficulty getting paid, except by the Archduke Rodolphe, who supported him for many years.

In the immediate future, the catalog continues to grow: the years 1809 and 1810 see the composition of the *Piano Concerto n° 5*, a virtuoso work created by Carl Czerny, the incidental music for Goethe's play *Egmont* and the *String Quartet n° 10,* known as *"The Harps*. Beethoven composed the *Sonata "Les Adieux"* for the imposed departure of his pupil and friend the Archduke Rudolf, the youngest son of the imperial family. The years 1811 and 1812 saw the composer reach the peak of his creative life. The *Archduke Trio* and the *Seventh* and *Eighth symphonies* are the high point of the heroic period.

On a personal level, Beethoven was deeply affected in 1810 by the failure of a marriage project with Therese Malfatti, the potential dedicatee of the famous *Letter to Elise*. Beethoven's love life has been the subject of much comment by his biographers. The composer fell in love with many beautiful women, most of them married, but he never experienced the marital happiness he was hoping for and which he praised in *Fidelio*. His love affairs with Giulietta Guicciardi (the inspiration for the Moonlight Sonata), Therese von Brunsvik (the dedicatee of the *Piano Sonata no.° 24*), Maria von Erdödy (who received the two *Cello Sonatas opus 102*) and Amalie Sebald remained short-lived experiences. Apart from the failure of this marriage project, the other major event in the musician's love life was the writing, in 1812, of the moving Lettre à l'immortelle Bien-aimée, whose dedicatee remains unknown, even if the names of Joséphine von Brunsvik and above all Antonia Brentano, are the ones that stand out most clearly in the study by Jean and Brigitte Massin and Maynard Solomon.

1813-1817: the dark years

The month of July 1812, abundantly commented on by the musician's biographers, marks a new turning point in Beethoven's life. While taking a spa treatment in the region of Teplitz and Carlsbad, he wrote the enigmatic *Letter to the Immortal Beloved* and met Goethe through Bettina Brentano. For reasons that remain unclear, this was also the beginning of a long period of sterility in the musician's creative life. It is known that the years that followed 1812 coincided with several dramatic events in Beethoven's life, events that he had to overcome alone, since almost all of his friends had left Vienna during the war of 1809, but nothing fully explains this break after ten years of such fertility.

In spite of the very favorable reception given by the public to the *Seventh Symphony* and to *Wellington's Victory* (December 1813), in spite of the finally triumphant revival of *Fidelio* in its definitive version (May 1814), Beethoven lost little by little the favor of Vienna, still nostalgic for Mozart and acquired to the lighter music of Rossini. The fuss made around the Congress of Vienna, where Beethoven was praised as a national musician, did not mask for long the growing condescension of the Viennese towards him. Moreover, the hardening of the regime imposed by Metternich placed him in a delicate situation, the Viennese police having long been aware of the democratic and revolutionary convictions of which the composer hid less and less. On a personal level, the major event is the death of his brother Kaspar-Karl on November 15, 1815. Beethoven, who had promised to direct the education of his son Karl, had to face an endless series of lawsuits against his sister-in-law to obtain the exclusive guardianship of his nephew, finally won in 1820. Despite the composer's good will and attachment, this nephew was to become for him, until the eve of his death, an inexhaustible source of torment. From these dark years, when his deafness became total, only a few rare masterpieces emerged: the *Cello Sonatas n° 4 and 5* dedicated to his confidante Maria von Erdödy (1815), the *Piano Sonata n° 28* (1816) and the cycle of lieder *To the Distant Beloved* (*An die ferne Geliebte*, 1815-1816), on poems by Alois Jeitteles (de).

While his material situation becomes more and more worrying, Beethoven falls seriously ill between 1816 and 1817 and seems once again close to suicide. However, his moral strength and willpower once again take over, with the support and friendship of the piano maker Nannette Streicher. Turning to introspection and spirituality, sensing the importance of what he still had to write for "the times to come", he found the strength to overcome these trials to begin a final creative period that would probably bring him his greatest revelations. Nine years before the premiere of the *Ninth Symphony*, Beethoven summed up in one sentence what would become in many ways his life's work (1815):

"We, limited beings with infinite minds, are only born for joy and for suffering. And one might almost say that the most eminent ones take hold of joy by going through suffering (*Durch Leiden, Freude*)."

Beethoven

1818-1827: the last Beethoven

Beethoven's strength returned at the end of 1817, when he sketched out a new sonata for the latest fortepiano

(*Hammerklavier* in German), which he considered to be the largest of all those he had composed up to that point. The *Grand Sonata for Hammerklavier,* Op. 106, exploits the instrument's possibilities to the limit, lasting nearly fifty minutes, and leaves Beethoven's contemporaries indifferent, judging it to be unplayable and believing that the musician's deafness made it impossible for him to properly appreciate its sound possibilities. With the exception of the *Ninth Symphony, the same is true* for all of the master's last works, which he himself was aware were far ahead of their time. Unconcerned with the complaints of performers, he declared to his publisher in 1819: "Here is a sonata that will give the pianists plenty of work when it is played in fifty years. From that time on, confined in his deafness, he had to communicate with his entourage through conversation notebooks which, although a large part of them has been destroyed or lost, constitute today an irreplaceable testimony on this last period. While it is known that he used a wooden stick between his teeth, leaning on the body of the piano to feel the vibrations, the anecdote of the sawn-off piano legs is historically less certain: the composer would have sawn off these legs in order to be able to play sitting on the floor to perceive the vibrations of the sounds transmitted by the floor.

Beethoven had always been a believer, without being a regular churchgoer, but his Christian fervor increased significantly after these difficult years, as shown by the numerous quotations of a religious nature that he copied into his notebooks from 1817 onwards. The rumors that he belonged to the Freemasonry have never been proven.

In the spring of 1818, he had the idea of a great religious work, which he initially envisaged as an enthronement mass for Archduke Rudolf, who was to be elevated to the rank of Archbishop of Olmütz a few months later. But the colossal *Missa solemnis* in D major required four years of hard work (1818-1822), and the mass was not delivered to its dedicatee until 1823. Beethoven studied Bach's masses and Handel's *Messiah* at length during the composition of the *Missa solemnis,* which he declared on several occasions to be "his best work, his greatest work. At the same time, he composed his last three *piano sonatas* (no.° 30, no.° 31 and no.° 32), the last of which, opus 111, ends with a highly spiritual *arietta* with variations that could have been his last piano work. But he still had to compose a final piano masterpiece: in 1822, the publisher Anton Diabelli invited all the composers of his time to write a variation on a very simple waltz of his composition. After initially mocking this waltz, Beethoven went beyond the proposed goal and produced a collection of *33 Variations* that Diabelli himself considered comparable to Bach's famous *Goldberg Variations*, composed eighty years earlier.

The *Ninth Symphony* and the last quartets

The composition of the *Ninth Symphony* began the day after the completion of the *Missa solemnis*, but the genesis of this work is extremely complex, and in order to understand it, one must go back to Beethoven's youth, when, even before his departure from Bonn, he planned to set Schiller's *Ode to Joy to music.* Through its unforgettable *finale* where choirs are introduced, an innovation in symphonic writing, the *Ninth Symphony* appears, in the tradition of the *Fifth*, as a musical evocation of the triumph of joy and brotherhood over despair, and takes on the dimension of a humanist and universal message. The symphony was premiered in front of an enthusiastic audience on May 7, 1824, and Beethoven returned to success for a time. It was in Prussia and England, where the musician's reputation had long been commensurate with his genius, that the symphony enjoyed its most dazzling success. Several times invited to London, as had Joseph Haydn, Beethoven was tempted towards the end of his life to travel to England, a country he admired for its cultural life and its democracy, and which he systematically opposed to the frivolity of Viennese life, But this project will not be realized and Beethoven will never know the country of his idol Handel, whose influence is particularly sensitive in the late period of Beethoven, who composes in his style, between 1822 and 1823, the overture *The Consecration of the House*.

The last five *String Quartets* (no.° 12, no.° 13, no.° 14, no.° 15, no.° 16) bring Beethoven's musical output to a close. By their visionary character, reviving old forms (use of the Lydian mode in the *Quartet n° 15*), they mark the culmination of Beethoven's research in chamber music. The large slow movements with a dramatic content (*Cavatine* in the *Quartet n° 13*, *Song of sacred thanksgiving of a convalescent to the Divinity* in the *Quartet n° 15*) announce the approaching romanticism. To these five quartets, composed in the period 1824-1826, one must add the *Great Fugue* in B flat major, opus 133, which was originally the concluding movement of the *Quartet n° 13*, but which Beethoven separated at the request of his publisher. At the end of the summer of 1826, while completing his *Quartet n° 16*, Beethoven was still planning many works: a *Tenth Symphony*, of which some sketches exist; an overture on the name of Bach; a *Faust* inspired by Goethe's play; an oratorio on the theme of Saul and David, another on the theme of the *Elements*; a *Requiem*. But on July 30, 1826, his nephew Karl attempted suicide. The affair caused a scandal, and Beethoven, distraught, left to rest at his brother Johann's in Gneixendorf in the region of Krems-on-the-Danube, in the company of his convalescent nephew. It was there

The end

Back in Vienna in December 1826, Beethoven contracted a double pneumonia from which he could not recover: the last four months of his life were marked by permanent pain and a terrible physical deterioration.

The direct cause of the musician's death, according to the observations of his last doctor, Dr. Wawruch, seems to be a decompensation of hepatic cirrhosis. Various causes have since been proposed: alcoholic cirrhosis, syphilis, acute hepatitis, sarcoidosis, Whipple's disease, Crohn's disease'.

Another controversial hypothesis is that Beethoven may also have suffered from Paget's disease (according to an autopsy performed in Vienna on March 27, 1827 by Karl Rokitansky, which mentions a uniformly dense and thick cranial vault and degenerated auditory nerves). The musician suffered from deformities consistent with Paget's disease; his head seems to have continued to grow in adulthood (by the end of his life, he could no longer fit into his hat or shoes); his forehead became prominent, his jaw was large, and his chin protruded. It is possible that compression of certain cranial nerves, especially the auditory nerve (eighth cranial nerve), affected his hearing; this is one of the hypotheses retrospectively brought forward to explain his mood and his deafness (which began around the age of twenty-seven and was total at forty-four).

But the most recent explanation, based on analyses of his hair and bone fragments, is that he suffered throughout his life (apart from his deafness, the composer regularly complained of abdominal pain and vision problems) from chronic lead poisoning combined with a genetic defect that prevented him from eliminating the lead absorbed by his body. The most probable origin of this lead poisoning is the consumption of wine. Beethoven, a great lover of Rhine wine and cheap "Hungarian wine", used to drink these wines "sweetened" at the time with lead salt in a lead crystal cup.

Until the end, the composer remained surrounded by his close friends, notably Karl Holz, Anton Schindler and Stephan von Breuning. A few weeks before his death, he received a visit from Franz Schubert, whom he did not know and regretted discovering so late. He sent his last letter to his friend, the composer Ignaz Moscheles, promoter of his music in London, in which he promised the English to compose a new symphony to thank them for their support. But on March 26, 1827, Ludwig van Beethoven died at the age of fifty-six. While Vienna had not cared much about his fate for months, his funeral, on March 29, 1827, brought together an impressive procession of several thousand anonymous people. Beethoven is buried in the central cemetery of Vienna.

"He knows everything, but we cannot understand everything yet, and there will be much water flowing in the Danube before everything this man has created is universally understood."

- Schubert, in 1827.

The Beethovenian *myth*

During his lifetime, Beethoven was already a myth, what we would call today a "cult" composer. Crossing artistic genres, going beyond cultural and geographical borders, he became at the same time the sign of a tradition and the symbol of a constantly renewed modernity.

"Legend always ends up being right against history, and the creation of myth is the ultimate victory of art."

- Emmanuel Buenzod, Power of Beethoven; Letters and music. Edition A. Corréa, 1936.

The musician of the German people

While in France, the *Beethoven myth* was only situated on the musical and ethical level, developing the image of a republican musician for the people, or animated by an absolute aesthetic requirement - with his quartets in particular - for the beautiful souls, it was different in Germany for obvious political reasons.

After the constitution of the German Reich on January 18, 1871, Beethoven was designated as one of the fundamental elements of the national heritage and of the national Kulturkampf. Bismarck confessed his predilection for a composer who gave him a healthy energy. From then on, Beethoven's music was heard alongside the nationalist song *Die Wacht am Rhein*.

In 1840, Richard Wagner had written an interesting short story, *A Visit to Beethoven*, an *episode in the life of a German musician*, in which he put himself in the shoes of a young composer who met Beethoven the day after the premiere of *Fidelio* and had the "great deaf man" develop very Wagnerian ideas about opera. Wagner, therefore, helped to establish Beethoven as the great musician of the German people.

In 1871, the year of the founding of the Reich, he published his account. It is known that in 1872 he celebrated the laying of the foundation stone of the *Bayreuther Festspielhaus* with a concert at the Margraves' Opera House in Bayreuth, during which he conducted the *Ninth Symphony*. A whole program, a whole lineage.

Paradoxically, the Beethovenian legacy fell into hands that were not necessarily the best suited to receive it. The leading composers of the post-Beethoven generation, Robert Schumann, Felix Mendelssohn, could not constitute true heirs. Their aesthetic orientations were too far from the model. In a way, the same was true for Johannes Brahms, but he was summoned by the German musical establishment to assume the legacy. It was up to him to extend the symphonic heritage. He hesitated for a long time before completing his *First Symphony* in 1876, after two decades of fumbling with the great shadow. When it was premiered, it was called Beethoven's *"Tenth Symphony.* Seven years later, when his *Third Symphony* was known, it was referred to as *the "Eroica".*

A kind of musical nationalism created a false filiation between the three Bs:

1. Bach, the eternal father;

2. Beethoven, the hero;

3. Brahms, the brilliant heir.

This was not a gift for the latter, whose temperament was more inclined towards intimate lyricism and chiaroscuro. He was therefore somewhat condemned by the political and cultural zeitgeist to revive a composer whom he both admired deeply and feared.

Gustav Mahler, in a sense, marked the final stage of Beethovenian influence in Austria. While his language is far removed from that of his distant predecessor, the very nature of his symphonies extended his personal message. Beethoven wrote in the margin of the manuscript of the *Missa solemnis*; "From the heart, may it return to the heart." Mahler also noted his moods in the margins of his scores. In both cases, the music embraces the world and the human condition. His *Second Symphony* with its final chorus is a daughter of Beethoven's *Ninth.* His *Third* is a hymn to nature like the *Pastoral*. And finally, his *Sixth* evokes three times the blows of *Fate*.

A universal and humanistic aura

After Nazism, the *Beethoven myth* could no longer be the same, in order to return to the universal and humanist Beethoven. The first four notes of the *Fifth Symphony* had been associated by the Allies with victory according to the analogy of three short and one long notes of the Morse code of the letter V, the Roman numeral five of Winston Churchill's victorious V. After the end of hostilities, the theme of the *Ode to Joy was* chosen as the European anthem and recorded by the Berlin Philharmonic Orchestra and Herbert von Karajan, who in his youth had often conducted Beethoven in an entirely different context. But schoolchildren in many countries had long been singing the lovely, idealistic song: *"Oh, what a beautiful dream lights up my eyes/What a bright sun rises in the pure, wide skies,"* said the French school version by Maurice Bouchor. In 1955, for the reopening of the Wiener Staatsoper in Vienna, after the repairs following the serious damage caused by the Allied bombing, *Fidelio* was staged, a hymn to the resistance to barbarism and to freedom regained, which was not without some ambiguity in a country that had been enthusiastic about the Anschluss, not to mention the conductor Karl Böhm, who had had some regrettable complacency with regard to the fallen regime.

The second half of the XXe century never ceased to celebrate Beethoven, who remained for a long time the leading composer of classical music. He often appears in the soundtracks of films, and in a particularly impressive way in Stanley Kubrick's *Clockwork Orange* (1971) where the distorted *Scherzo* of the *Ninth Symphony* represents the deviant energy of Alex, the psychopathic hero. However, in recent decades, the wave of return to early music and a certain distrust of sentiment and emphatic exaltation have lowered Beethoven's profile. The use of period instruments and different performance practices allowed for a new sound image.

Emil Cioran suggests that this intimate and grandiose way of approaching music - which is mainly the work of commentators after Beethoven - had "vitiated" its evolution. Yehudi Menuhin considers that with Beethoven, music begins to change its nature and move towards a kind of moral control over the listener. A sort of totalitarian power. This was a century earlier the point of view of Leo Tolstoy in his short story *The Kreutzer Sonata*, which associates the love of music with a sickly passion.

The icon of freedom

In any case, globally, the image that remains is that of a militant for freedom, human rights and social progress.

On December 25, 1989, Leonard Bernstein conducts the *Ninth Symphony in* front of the dismantled Berlin Wall and replaces the word "*Freude*" (joy) in the *Ode* with "*Freiheit*" (freedom). Deutsche Grammophon commercialized the recording of the concert by inserting a piece of the real wall in the box as an anti-relic.

The meaning of these events, however, is rather vague. In 1981, during the inauguration ceremony of François Mitterrand, Daniel Barenboim, with the choirs and the Orchestre de Paris, performed the last movement of the *Ninth in* front of the Pantheon.

In 1995, Jean-Marie Le Pen opened the meeting in which he announced his candidacy for the presidential election, with *the Ode to Joy*. In November 2015, to cover a demonstration of a far-right movement protesting against immigration, the choirs of the Mainz Opera sing this hymn.

Flash mobs on the *Ode to Joy* - a modern practice, rather light and consensual, but significant all the same -, in the Sant Roc square in Sabadell, in front of the Saint Lawrence church in Nuremberg, in Tokushima' , in Fukushima, in Hong Kong, in Odessa or in Tunis, express the desire for freedom of a young crowd. In these contexts, Beethoven is sought after.

In the introduction to his *Mythologies*, Roland Barthes wrote this famous and enigmatic sentence: *"A myth is a word.* Polysemic, versatile, flexible, this word lives with time, lives with its time. The current Beethoven of the *flashmobs* is far from the inner fire that animates the busts of Antoine Bourdelle, from the somewhat emphatic humanism of Romain Rolland or from the nationalist claims of the two Reichs. It is the proof, by the movement, that the myth still runs.

Musical style and innovations

Youth in Bonn

[e]Contrary to popular belief, the first musical influences on the young Beethoven were not so much those of Haydn or Mozart - whose music, with the exception of a few scores, he did not really discover until he arrived in Vienna - as those of the gallant style of the second half of the 18th century and of the composers of the Mannheim School, whose works he could hear in Bonn, at the court of Elector Maximilian Francis of Austria.

The works from this period do not appear in the opus catalog. They were composed between 1782 and 1792 and already show a remarkable mastery of composition; but his personality does not yet manifest itself as it will in the Viennese period.

The *Sonatas for the Elector* WoO 47 (1783), the *Piano Concerto* WoO 4 (1784) and the *Piano Quartets* WoO 36 (1785) are strongly influenced by the gallant style of composers such as Johann Christian Bach.

that he wrote his last work, an *allegro* to replace the
Great Fugue as the finale of the *Quartet n° 13*.

Two other members of the Bach family formed the basis of the young Beethoven's musical culture:

- Carl Philipp Emanuel Bach, whose sonatas he plays;

- Johann Sebastian Bach, whose two books of the *Well-Tempered Clavier* he learned by heart.

In both cases, it is more a question of studies intended for the mastery of one's instrument than for composition itself.

The decisive influence of Haydn

The particularity of Haydn's influence - compared to that of Clementi in particular - is that it literally goes beyond the simple aesthetic domain (to which it applies only momentarily and superficially) to permeate the very foundation of Beethoven's conception of music. Indeed, the model of the Viennese master does not manifest itself so much, as is too often believed, in the works known as "of the first period," as in those of the following years: the *Eroica Symphony*, in its spirit and proportions, has much more to do with Haydn than the two preceding ones; in the same way, Beethoven is closer to his elder in his last quartet, completed in 1826, than in his first, composed some thirty years earlier. One can thus distinguish, in Haydn's style, the aspects that will become essential to the Beethovenian spirit.

More than anything else, it is the Haydnian sense of motif that has had a profound and lasting influence on Beethoven's work. Never has Beethoven's work known a more fundamental and immutable principle than that of building an entire movement from a thematic cell - sometimes reduced to the extreme - and the most famous masterpieces bear witness to this, as in the first movement of the *Fifth Symphony*. The quantitative reduction of the starting material must be matched by an extension of the development; and if the impact of Haydn's innovation has been so great, on Beethoven and thus indirectly on the whole history of music, it is precisely because the Haydnian motif was intended to generate a thematic development of a hitherto unheard-of scope.

This influence of Haydn is not always limited to the theme or even to its development, but sometimes extends to the internal organization of an entire sonata movement. For the master of Viennese classicism, it is the thematic material that determines the form of the work. Here again, more than an influence, one can speak of a principle that will become truly substantial in the Beethovenian spirit, and that the composer will develop even more than his elder in his most accomplished productions. Thus it is, for example, as Charles Rosen explains, in the first movement of the "Hammerklavier" *Sonata*: it is the descending third of the main theme that determines the entire structure (for example, throughout the piece, the keys follow one another in an order of descending thirds: B-flat major, G major, E-flat major, B major...)

Apart from these essential aspects, other less fundamental features of Haydn's work sometimes influenced Beethoven. A few earlier examples could be cited, but Haydn was the first composer to actually use a technique of beginning a piece in a false key - that is, a key other than the tonic. This principle illustrates the typical Haydnian propensity to surprise the listener, a tendency that is widely found in Beethoven: the last movement of the *Fourth Piano Concerto*, for example, seems to begin in C major for a few bars before the tonic (G major) is clearly established. Haydn was also the first to address the issue of integrating the fugue into sonata form, which he addressed primarily by using the fugue as a development. In this field, before developing new methods (which will only be used in the *Piano Sonata n° 32* and the *String Quartet n° 14*), Beethoven will take up his master's ideas several times: the last movement of the *Piano Sonata n° 28* and the first movement of the Hammerklavier *Sonata* are probably the best examples.

And yet, despite the links noted by musicologists between the two composers, Beethoven, who admired Cherubini and venerated Handel ("I would have liked to kneel before the great Handel"), and seemed to have appreciated Salieri's lessons more, did not understand him in this way and did not recognize Haydn's influence. He declared that he had "never learned anything from Haydn" according to Ferdinand Ries, friend and pupil of Beethoven.

The influence of Mozart

Even more than before, we must distinguish between Mozart's influence on Beethoven and his formal influence. The Mozartian aesthetic is mainly manifested in the works of the so-called "first period", and this in a rather superficial way, since the influence of the master is most often limited to borrowing ready-made formulas. Until around 1800, Beethoven's music was mainly in the sometimes post-classical, sometimes pre-romantic style represented by composers such as Clementi or Hummel; a style that only imitates Mozart on the surface, and that could be described more as "classicizing" than as truly classical (according to Rosen's expression).

The formal - and more profound - aspect of Mozart's influence is more apparent in the works of the so-called "second period. It is in the concerto, a genre that Mozart brought to its highest level, that the master's model seems to have remained the most present. Thus, in the first movement of the *Piano Concerto No.º 4*, the abandonment of the double sonata exposition (successively orchestra and soloist) in favor of a single exposition (simultaneously orchestra and soloist) in a way repeats the Mozartian idea of merging the static presentation of the theme (orchestra) into its dynamic presentation (soloist). More generally, Beethoven, in his propensity to amplify the codas to the point of transforming them into fully-fledged thematic elements, is much more the heir of Mozart than of Haydn - in whom the codas are much less distinct from the recapitulation.

Some of Mozart's pieces remind us of great pages of Beethoven's work, the two most striking are: the offertory K 222 composed in 1775 (violins starting at about 1 minute) which strongly reminds us of the theme of the Ode to Joy, the 4 strokes of the timpani of the 1er movement of the piano concerto n°25 written in 1786 reminding us of the famous introduction of the 5^{e} symphony.

Clementi's piano sonatas

In the field of piano music, it is above all the influence of Muzio Clementi that quickly exerts itself on Beethoven from 1795 and allows his personality to assert itself and truly blossom. Although not as profound as Haydn's works, the influence of the famous editor's piano sonatas was nonetheless immense in Beethoven's stylistic evolution, and he judged them to be superior to Mozart's. Some of them, because of the way they are written, are not only the most important works of Beethoven, but also the most important. Some of the sonatas, with their boldness, emotional power, and innovative treatment of the instrument, inspired some of Beethoven's early masterpieces, and the elements that first set the composer's piano style apart came largely from Clementi.

Thus, as early as the 1780s, Clementi made new use of chords that had been little used until then: octaves, mainly, but also sixths and parallel thirds. In this way, he significantly fleshed out piano writing, endowing the instrument with an unprecedented sonic power, which certainly impressed the young Beethoven, who quickly integrated these procedures into his own style in his first three sonatas. The use of dynamic indications expands in Clementi's sonatas: *pianissimo* and *fortissimo* become frequent and their expressive function takes on considerable importance. Here too, Beethoven grasped the possibilities opened up by these innovations, and as early as the "Pathetique" Sonata, these principles were definitively integrated into the Beethovenian style.

Another point in common between Beethoven's first sonatas and those - contemporary or earlier - of Clementi is their length, relatively important for the time: the sonatas of Clementi, from which the young Beethoven drew his inspiration, are indeed large-scale works, often consisting of vast movements. We find in them the beginnings of a new vision of the musical work, henceforth conceived to be unique. Beethoven's piano sonatas are known as his "experimental laboratory," from which he drew new ideas that he later extended to other forms, such as the symphony. Through them, Clementi's influence was thus felt throughout Beethoven's output. Thus, as Marc Vignal points out, one finds, for example, important influences from Clementi's sonatas op. 13 n° 6 and op. 34 n° 2 in the *Eroica Symphony*.

The heroic style and its inspirers

Once the "heroic" influences had been assimilated, once he had truly taken the "new path" he wished to follow, and once he had definitively asserted his personality through the achievements of a creative period extending from the *Eroica Symphony* to the *Seventh Symphony*, Beethoven ceased to be interested in the works of his contemporaries, and consequently to be influenced by them. Among his contemporaries, only Cherubini and Schubert still enchanted him; but in no way did he think of imitating them. Despising Italian opera above all else, and strongly disapproving of the emerging Romanticism, Beethoven felt the need to turn to the historical "pillars" of music: J.S. Bach and G.F. Handel, as well as the great masters of the Renaissance, such as Palestrina. Among these influences, Handel's place is more than privileged: he probably never had a more fervent admirer than

Beethoven, who (pointing to his complete works, which he had just received) exclaimed: "Here is the truth!"; or Beethoven who, in the evening of his life, said he wanted to "kneel on his grave.

Of Handel's work, the music of the later Beethoven often takes on a grandiose and generous aspect, through the use of dotted rhythms - as is the case in the introduction to the *Piano Sonata no.º 32*, in the first movement of the *Ninth Symphony*, or in the second *Diabelli Variation* - or even through a certain sense of harmony, as is shown by the opening bars of the second movement of the *Piano Sonata no.º 30*, entirely harmonized in the purest Handelian style.

It is also the inexhaustible vitality characteristic of Handel's music that fascinates Beethoven, and which is found, for example, in the choral fugato on "Freude, schöner Götterfunken" that follows the famous "Seid umschlungen, Millionen" in the finale of the *Ninth Symphony*: the theme that appears there, swayed by a powerful ternary rhythm, is typically Handelian in its simplicity and liveliness, right down to its slightest melodic contours. A new step is taken with the *Missa solemnis*, where the mark of Handel's great choral works is felt more than ever. Beethoven is so absorbed in the world of the *Messiah* that he transcribes note for note one of the most famous motifs of the *Halleluja* in the

Gloria. In other works, the nervousness of Handel's dotted rhythms is perfectly integrated into Beethoven's style, as in the effervescent *Grande Fugue* or in the second movement of the *Piano Sonata no.º 32*, where this influence is gradually transformed.

Finally, it is also in the field of the fugue that Handel's work permeates Beethoven. If the examples of the genre written by the author of *Messiah* are based on a perfect mastery of contrapuntal techniques, they are generally based on simple themes and follow a path that does not pretend to the extreme elaboration of Bach's fugues. This must have satisfied Beethoven, who, on the one hand, shares Handel's concern for building entire works from material that is as simple and reduced as possible, and who, on the other hand, does not possess the predisposition for counterpoint that would allow him to seek excessive sophistication.

The style

A classical composer

The three "ways" are a progression of the child learning, becoming an adult and being deified:

1. 1793-1801: the period of imitation in form: the piano style of Carl P. E. Bach according to the creative idea of Friedrich Wilhelm Rust in an architecture of Haydn;

2. 1801-1815: the period of transition: the love of *the* woman - Juliette Guicciardi -, of the nature and the fatherland;

3. 1815-1827: the period of reflection.

The heritage in the XIX[e] century

The last great representative of Viennese classicism (after Gluck, Haydn and Mozart), Beethoven paved the way for the evolution of romanticism in music and influenced Western music for a large part of the XIX[e] century. Unclassifiable ("You give me the impression of a man with many heads, many hearts, many souls," said Haydn to him around 1793), his art was expressed through different musical genres, and although his symphonic music is the main source of his popularity, he also had a considerable impact in piano writing and chamber music.

Beethoven in the XX[e] century

It is in the XX[e] century that Beethoven's music found its greatest interpreters. It occupies a central place in the repertoire of most of the pianists and concert artists of the century (Kempff, Richter, Nat, Arrau, Ney, Rubinstein...) and a certain number of them, following Artur Schnabel, recorded the complete piano sonatas. The orchestral work, already recognized since the 19th century[e] , reached its peak with the interpretations of Herbert von Karajan and Wilhelm Furtwängler.

"In music,] behind the non-rational rhythms, there is the primitive "intoxication" definitively rebellious to any articulation; behind the rational articulation, there is the "form" which, on its side, has the will and the force to absorb and to order all life, and thus finally the intoxication itself! It is Nietzsche who, for the first time, formulated this duality in a grandiose way thanks to the concepts of Dionysian and Apollonian. But for us, today, who consider Beethoven's music, it is a matter of realizing that these two elements are not contradictory - or, rather, that they do not have to be. It seems to be the task of art, of art in Beethoven's sense, to reconcile them."

- Wilhelm Furtwängler, 1951.

And in 1942:

"Beethoven contains within himself the whole nature of man. He is not essentially singing like Mozart, he does not have the architectural élan of Bach nor the dramatic sensualism of Wagner. He unites all of this in himself, each thing being in its place: there lies the essence of his originality. [...] Never has a musician better felt and expressed the harmony of the spheres, the song of Divine Nature. Only through him, Schiller's lines: "*Brothers, above the vault of stars / Must reign a loving father*" have found their living reality, which goes far beyond what words can express."

He concluded in 1951:

"Thus, Beethoven's music remains for us a great example of unanimous agreement where all tendencies meet, an example of harmony between the language of the soul, between the musical architecture and the unfolding of a drama rooted in the psychic life, but above all between the Ego and Humanity, between the anxious soul of the isolated individual, and the community in its universality. The words of Schiller: "*Brothers, above the vault of stars / Must reign a loving father*", that Beethoven proclaimed with a divinatory clarity in the message of his last symphony, were not in his mouth words of preacher or demagogue; it is what he himself lived concretely throughout his life, since the beginning of his artistic activity. And this is also the reason why we, today's men, are still so deeply touched by such a message."

It is also necessary to wait until the XXe century for certain scores like the *Diabelli Variations* or the *9^e symphony to* be re-studied and reconsidered by the musical world.

Beethoven in the XXIe century

Nowadays, Beethoven's message seems to be surprisingly relevant and the success of his music is never denied.

Instruments

One of Beethoven's pianos was an instrument made by the Viennese company Geschwister Stein. On November 19, 1796, Beethoven wrote a letter to Andreas Streicher, the husband of Nannette Streicher: *"I received your pianoforte the day before yesterday. It is really wonderful, anyone would like to have it for himself..."*

As Carl Czerny recalls, in 1801 Beethoven had a Walter piano in his house. In 1802 he also asked his friend Zmeskall to ask Walter to build him a one-string pianoforte.

Then, in 1803, Beethoven received his Erard grand piano. But, as Newman writes: *"Beethoven was not satisfied with this instrument from the start, partly because the composer found its English action incurably heavy.*

Another piano by Beethoven, the Broadwood 1817, was a gift from Thomas Broadwood. Beethoven kept it at his home in the Schwarzspanierhaus until his death in 1827.

Beethoven's last instrument was a four-string Graf piano. Conrad Graf himself confirmed that he loaned Beethoven a 6 ½ octave piano, and then sold it, after the composer's death, to the Wimmer family. In 1889, the instrument was acquired by the Beethovenhaus in Bonn.

The work of Beethoven

In musical history, Beethoven's work represents a transition between the classical era (approximately 1750-1810) and the romantic era (approximately 1810-1900). If his early works are influenced by Haydn or Mozart, his mature works are rich in innovations and opened the way to musicians with an exacerbated romanticism, such as Brahms (whose First Symphony evokes Beethoven's "Tenth" according to Hans von Bulow, probably because of its finale in which Brahms voluntarily introduces a theme close to that of the Ode to Joy in homage to the Master), Schubert, Wagner and Bruckner:

- the opening of his *Fifth Symphony* (1807), exposes a violent motif - an omnipresent motif from his early works - which is reused throughout the four movements; the transition from the third to the last movement is *attacca* (without interruption);

- the *Ninth Symphony* (1824) is the first symphony to introduce a chorus, in the fourth movement. The whole orchestral treatment represents a real innovation; let us add that the mysterious introduction of 16 bars, with tonal uncertainty (only the three notes A, D, E are used, we therefore know neither the key nor the mode, major or minor) which opens the symphony, will inspire Bruckner whose *Eighth symphony* includes an inversion of the places of the Scherzo and the Adagio as in Beethoven's *Ninth*;

- His opera, *Fidelio*, uses the voices as symphonic instruments, without regard to the technical limitations of the chorus.

In terms of musical technique, the use of motifs that feed entire movements is considered a major contribution. Essentially rhythmic in nature - which is a great novelty - these motifs are modified and multiplied to form developments. This is the case for the very famous :

- first movement of the *Fourth Piano Concerto* (given from the first bars) ;

- first movement of the *Fifth Symphony* (*idem*) ;

- The second movement of the *Seventh Symphony* (in dactylic rhythm): the ever-renewed whirlwind that results is extremely striking, at the origin of this great vehemence that constantly "comes" for the listener.

Beethoven was also one of the very first to take such care with the orchestration. In the developments, changing associations, especially among the woodwinds, allow for a singular illumination of the thematic returns, which are also slightly modified on the harmonic level. The variations of tone and color that follow renew the discourse while preserving the reference points of memory.

If Beethoven's works are so appreciated, it is also because of their emotional force, characteristic of Romanticism.

The general public is most familiar with his symphonic works, which are often innovative, especially the Sixth, known as the *Pastoral*, and the "odd" symphonies: 3, 5, 7 and 9. His best-known concertante works are the *Violin Concerto* and especially the *Fifth Piano Concerto*, known as *The Emperor*. His instrumental music is appreciated through some magnificent piano sonatas, among the thirty-two he wrote. His chamber music, including 16 string quartets, is less well known.

There are 398 works by Beethoven.

Symphonic works

Haydn composed over one hundred symphonies and Mozart over forty. From his predecessors, Beethoven did not inherit productivity, for he composed only nine symphonies, and sketched out a tenth. But Beethoven's nine symphonies are far more monumental and all have their own identity. Curiously, several Romantic or post-romantic composers died after their ninth (completed or not), hence a curse legend attached to this number:

Schubert, Bruckner, Dvořák, Mahler, but also Ralph Vaughan Williams.

Beethoven's first two symphonies are classically inspired and constructed. However, the *3ᵉ symphony*, known as the "*Eroica*", will mark a great turning point in orchestral composition. Much more ambitious than its predecessors, the *Eroica* stands out for the size of its movements and the treatment of the orchestra. The first movement alone is longer than most symphonies written at that time. This monumental work, originally written as a tribute to Napoleon Bonaparte before he was crowned emperor, reveals Beethoven as a great musical architect and is considered the first proven example of Romanticism in music.

Although it is shorter and often considered more classical than its predecessor, the dramatic tensions that punctuate it make the *4ᵉ symphony* a logical step in Beethoven's stylistic development. Then come two monuments created the same evening, the *5ᵉ symphony* and the *6ᵉ symphony*. The Fifth, with its famous four-note motive, often referred to as the "fate motive" (the composer is said to have said, when speaking of this famous theme, that it represents "fate knocking at the door"), can be compared to the Third by its monumental aspect. Another innovative aspect is the repeated use of the four-note motif on which most of the symphony is based. The 6^e *symphony, known as the "Pastoral"* *symphony*, wonderfully evokes the nature that Beethoven loved so much. In addition to peaceful, dreamy moments, the symphony has a movement where the music paints a most realistic storm.

The 7^e *symphony* is, in spite of a second movement in the form of a funeral march, marked by its joyful aspect and the frenetic rhythm of its finale, described by Richard Wagner as the "Apotheosis of the dance. The following symphony, brilliant and spiritual, returns to a more classical style. Finally, the *Ninth Symphony* is the last completed symphony and the jewel in the crown. Over an hour long, it is a symphony in four movements that does not respect sonata form. Each of them is a masterpiece of composition which shows that Beethoven has completely freed himself from classical conventions and has opened up new perspectives in the treatment of the orchestra. It is to his last movement that Beethoven adds a chorus and a vocal quartet that sing the *Ode to Joy*, a poem by Friedrich von Schiller. This work calls for love and brotherhood among all men, and the score is now part of UNESCO's World Heritage List. The *Ode to Joy was* chosen as the European anthem.

Concertos and concertante works

At the age of 14, Beethoven had already written a modest Piano Concerto in E-flat major (WoO 4), which remained unpublished during his lifetime. Only the piano part remains, with rather rudimentary orchestral replicas. Seven years later, in 1791, two more concertos appear to have been among his most impressive achievements, but unfortunately nothing survives that can be attributed with certainty to the original version except for a fragment of the second violin concerto. Around 1800, he composed two romances for violin and orchestra (op. 40 and op. 50). But Beethoven remains above all a composer of piano concertos, works that he reserved for performance in concert - except for the last one, where, his deafness having become complete, he had to let his pupil Czerny play it on November 28, 1811 in Vienna. Of all the genres, the concerto is the one most marked by his deafness: indeed, he did not compose any more once he became deaf.

The most important concertos are the five for piano. Unlike Mozart's concertos, these are works written specifically for the piano, whereas Mozart allowed the harpsichord to be used. He was one of the first to compose exclusively for the fortepiano and thus imposed a new sound aesthetic on the solo concerto.

The numbering of the concertos respects the order of creation except for the first two. The first concerto was composed in 1795 and published in 1801, while the second concerto was composed earlier (around 1788), but only published in December 1801. However, the chronology remains unclear: at Beethoven's first major public concert, at the Hofburgtheater in Vienna, on March 29, 1795, a concerto was premiered, but it is not known whether it was his first or second. The composition of the *Third Concerto* took place during the period when he was completing his first quartets and his first two symphonies, as well as some large piano sonatas. He declares that he now knows how to write quartets and will now know how to write concertos. Its premiere took place during the great public concert in Vienna on April 5, 1803. The *Fourth Concerto was written* at a time when the composer was asserting himself in all genres, from the Razumovsky Quartets to the "Appassionata" Sonata, from the *Eroica Symphony* to his opera Leonor. Of these five concertos, the fifth is the most typical of the Beethovenian style. Subtitled "The Emperor" but not by the composer, it was composed in 1808, a period of political unrest whose traces can be found on its manuscript with annotations such as "Auf die Schlacht Jubelgesang" ("Triumphal song for the battle"), "Angriff" ("Attack"), "Sieg" ("Victory").

Beethoven's only *Violin Concerto* (op. 61) dates from 1806 and was commissioned by his friend Franz Clement. He made a transcription for piano, sometimes called the *Sixth* Piano *Concerto* (op. 61a). Beethoven also composed a *Triple Concerto for violin, cello and piano* (op. 56) in 1803-1804.

In 1808, Beethoven wrote a Choral Fantasy for piano, choir and orchestra, Op. 80, which is part sonata, part concerto and part choral work, one of the themes of which was to become the basis of the *Ode to Joy*.

Music for the stage

Beethoven wrote three stage scores: *Egmont*, op. 84 (1810), *The Ruins of Athens*, op. 113 (1811) and *King Stephen*, op. 117 (1811) and wrote a ballet: *The Creatures of Prometheus*, op. 43 (1801).

He also composed several overtures: *Leonore I*, op. 138 (1805), *Leonore II*, op. 72 (1805), *Leonore III*, op. 72a (1806), *Coriolan*, op. 62 (1807), *Le Roi Étienne*, op. 117 (1811), *Fidelio*, op. 72b (1814), *Jour de fête*, op. 115 (1815) and *La Conécration de la maison*, op. 124 (1822)

Finally, Beethoven wrote a single opera, *Fidelio*, a work to which he was most attached, and certainly the one that cost him the most effort. Indeed, this opera is built on the basis of a first attempt entitled *Leonore*, an opera that was not well received by the public. Nevertheless, there are still three versions of the opening of *Leonore*, the last one being often performed before the finale of *Fidelio*.

Music for piano

Although the symphonies are his most popular works and the ones by which Beethoven's name is known to the general public, it is certainly in his music for the piano (as well as for the string quartet) that Beethoven's genius is most apparent.

Recognized early on as a master in the art of touching the fortepiano, the composer was to take a close interest in all the technical developments of the instrument in order to exploit all its possibilities.

Sonatas for piano

Traditionally, Beethoven is said to have written 32 piano sonatas, but in reality there are 35 fully completed piano sonatas. The first three are the piano sonatas WoO 47, composed in 1783 and known as the *Elector Sonatas*. As for the 32 traditional sonatas, works of major importance for Beethoven since he gave an opus number to each of them, their composition is spread over a period of twenty years. This set, now considered one of the monuments dedicated to the instrument, bears witness, even more than the symphonies, to the stylistic development of the composer over the years. The sonatas, in classical form at the beginning, will gradually free themselves from this form and keep only the name, Beethoven enjoying beginning or ending a composition with a slow movement, for example in the famous Moonlight Sonata, or adding a fugue (see the last movement of the *Sonata n⁰ 31* in *A* flat major, op. 110), or to call a two-movement composition a sonata (see *Sonatas n⁰ 19* and *20*, op. *49*, 1-2).

As time went on, the compositions gained in freedom of writing, became more and more structured and complex. Among the most famous are the *Appassionata* (1804), the *Waldstein* of the same year, and *Les Adieux* (1810). In the famous *Hammerklavier* (1819), the length and technical difficulties reach such proportions that they challenge the physical possibilities of the performer as well as those of the instrument, and demand sustained attention from the listener. It is one of the last five sonatas, which form a separate group known as the "last manner". This term designates a stylistic culmination of Beethoven's work, in which the composer, now totally deaf and in possession of all the technical difficulties of composition, abandons all formal considerations in order to focus solely on invention and the discovery of new sound territories. The last five sonatas constitute a high point in the piano literature. Beethoven's "last manner", associated with the last period of the master's life, designates the most acute manifestation of his genius and will have no descendants, except perhaps for ragtime (arrietta, sonata no. 32).

In addition to the 32 sonatas, there are the *Bagatelles*, the numerous series of variations, various works, notably the rondos op. 51, as well as a few pieces for piano four hands.

Bagatelles

The bagatelles are short pieces, strongly contrasted, often published in collections. The first collection opus 33, gathered in 1802 and published in 1803 in Vienna, consists of seven bagatelles of a hundred measures each, all in major keys. The emphasis is on lyricism, as can be seen in the indication for the bagatelle n° 6: *con una certa espressione parlante* ("with a certain spoken expression").

The next collection, Opus 119, contains eleven bagatelles, but is in fact composed of two collections (bagatelles 1 to 6 on one side and 7 to 11 on the other). The second one was the first one, in 1820, at the request of his friend Friedrich Starke in order to contribute to a piano method. In 1822, the publisher Peters asked Beethoven for works. He collected five early pieces that had been composed many years earlier and reworked them in various ways. However, none of these five pieces presented a satisfactory conclusion for Beethoven, so he composed a sixth bagatelle. Peters refused to publish the set of six, and Clementi published it, adding the pieces written for Starke to make up the collection of eleven pieces as we know it today.

His last collection, Opus 126, is composed solely on new bases. It consists of six bagatelles composed in 1824. When Beethoven was working on this collection, there were five other completed bagatelles that now stand alone alongside the three collections. The best known, dating from 1810, is the *Letter to Elise* (WoO 59). The other four are: WoO 52, 56, the German 81 and Hess 69. Other small pieces can be considered as trifles as such, but they were never part of any plan by Beethoven to publish them in a collection.

Variations

The series of variations can be viewed period by period. He composed a total of twenty series of very diverse importance. Those of major importance to Beethoven are those for which he assigned an Opus number, namely: the six Variations on an original theme in D major op. 76, the six Variations on an original theme in F major op. 34 (variations on *The Ruins of Athens*), the *15 Variations* on the theme of The *Creatures of Prometheus* in E flat major, op. 35 (wrongly called Heroic Variations because the theme of The *Creatures of Prometheus* (op. 43) was taken up by Beethoven for the last movement of his Symphony no.° 3, "heroic". But the theme was originally composed for the ballet) and finally the monument of the genre, the *Diabelli Variations* opus 120.

The first period is the one when Beethoven is in Vienna. The first work ever published by Beethoven is the variations in C minor WoO 63. They were composed in 1782 (Beethoven was 11 years old). Before his departure for Vienna in 1792, Beethoven composed three other series (WoO 64 to 66).

Then came the years 1795-1800, during which Beethoven composed no less than nine sets (WoO 68-73 and 75-77). Most of them are based on arias from successful operas and singspiels, and almost all of them include a long coda in which the theme is developed rather than simply varied. It was also at this time that Beethoven began to use original themes for his series of variations.

Then came the year 1802, when Beethoven composed two more important and unusual series. These are the six variations in F major, op. 34, and the fifteen variations and fugue in E flat major, op. 35. As these are major works, he assigned them an opus number (none of the earlier series has an opus number). The original idea in Op. 34 was to write a varied theme in which each variation would have its own measure and tempo. He also decided to write each variation in a particular key. The theme was thus not only subjected to variation, but also underwent a complete transformation of character. Later composers such as Liszt would make great use of thematic transformation, but it was surprising in 1802. The variations, op. 35, are even more innovative. Here Beethoven uses a theme from the finale of his ballet *The Creatures of Prometheus*, a theme he also used in the finale of the "Eroica" Symphony, which gave the variations their name ("*eroica*"). The first innovation is found at the beginning, where, instead of stating his theme, Beethoven presents only the bass line in octaves, without accompaniment. This is followed by three variations in which the bass line is accompanied by one, two, and then three counterpoints, while the bass line appears in the bass, in the middle, and then in the treble. The true theme finally appears followed by 15 variations.

The series ends with a long fugue based on the first four notes of the starting bass line. This is followed by two more double variations before a brief final section that concludes the work.

The last period is from 1802 to 1809 when Beethoven composed four series (WoO 78 to 80 and op. 76). From 1803 on, he tended to concentrate on larger works (Symphonies, string quartets, incidental music). The first two of the four series listed, composed in 1803, are based on English melodies: *God Save the Queen* and *Rule, Britannia!* by Thomas Arne. The 3rd[e] was written in C minor on an original theme in 1806. The theme is distinguished by its extreme concentration: only eight measures. The measure remains unchanged in all 32 variations. With the exception of the middle section of five variations (no.[os] 12-16) in C major, it is the key of C minor that defines the mood of the work. Contrary to what some might expect, wanting to see this set among Beethoven's greatest works, the composer published it without an opus number or dedicatee. Its origins remain obscure. Then come the six variations in D major, Op. 76, composed in 1809 and dedicated to Franz Oliva, a friend of Beethoven's. He later reused the theme of the D major variations in 1809. He later reused the theme of this series in 1811 for the one-act *singspiel The Ruins of Athens*. Ten years passed before Beethoven wrote his last set of variations.

Finally, in 1822, the publisher and composer Anton Diabelli had the idea to gather in a collection pieces of the major composers of his time around a single musical theme of his own composition. The set of variations - called "Diabelli Variations" - was to serve as a musical panorama of the time. Beethoven, who had not written for the piano for a long time, took to the game, and instead of providing one variation, wrote 33, which were published in a separate booklet. The *Diabelli Variations*, because of their invention, constitute the true testament of Beethoven the pianist.

Minor" parts

Many other small pieces could have taken their place in the collections of bagatelles. One of them is the *rondo a capriccio* op. 129, which he composed in 1795 and which was found in his papers after his death, not quite finished. It was Diabelli who made the necessary additions and published it shortly afterwards under the title *La colère pour un sou perdu*. This title appeared on the original manuscript, but was not in Beethoven's hand, and it is not known whether it had the composer's approval. The other short pieces in the bagatelle style range from the Allegretto in C minor (WoO 53) to the tiny 13-bar Allegretto quasi andante in G minor (WoO 61a).

Other substantial pieces are the Andante Favori in F major (WoO 57) and the Fantasy in G minor (Op. 77). The andante was written as a slow movement for the "Dawn" sonata, but Beethoven replaced it with a much shorter movement. The fantasy is little known and yet is a rather extraordinary composition. It is sinuous and improvisatory in character: it begins with scales in G minor and after a series of interruptions ends with a theme and variations in the key of B major.

Finally, the two rondos op. 51, composed independently of each other and published in 1797 and 1802, are of comparable proportions to the andante and the fantasia. There are two other rondos (WoO 48 & 49) that Beethoven composed at the age of about 12.

Beethoven also composed dances for piano. These include the Scots and Waltzes WoO 83 to 86, the six minuets WoO 10, the seven ländler WoO 11 and the twelve allemandes WoO 12. There is, however, one important piece in the Polonaise in C major, Op. 89, which was composed in 1814 and dedicated to the Empress of Russia.

Pieces for piano 4 hands

There are very few works for piano four hands. They consist of two sets of variations, a sonata and three marches. The first set of variations (WoO 67) is based on a theme by the patron Waldstein. The second set of variations on his own lied "Ich denke dein" (WoO 74) was begun in 1799, when Beethoven composed the lied and four variations, and was published in 1805 after the addition of two more variations. The sonata op. 6 is in two movements and was composed around 1797. The marches (op. 45) were commissioned by Count Browne and written around 1803. Finally, Beethoven made a transcription of his "Great Fugue" opus 133 (op. 134) for piano duet. This was originally the finale of the string quartet op. 130, but the reviews were so bad that Beethoven was forced to rewrite another finale and the publisher had the idea of transcribing the original finale for piano four hands.

Pieces for organ

Beethoven wrote little for the organ, including a two-part fugue in D major (WoO 31) composed in 1783, two preludes for piano or organ (op. 39) composed in 1789, and pieces for a mechanical organ (WoO 33) composed in 1799. There are also works composed by Beethoven as part of his training with Neefe, Haydn and Albrechtsberger.

String quartets

The great monument of Beethoven's chamber music is formed by the 16 string quartets. It is undoubtedly for this formation that Beethoven entrusted his deepest inspirations. The string quartet was popularized by

Boccherini, Haydn and Mozart, but it was Beethoven who first made full use of the possibilities of this formation. The last six quartets, and the "Great Fugue" in particular, constitute the unsurpassed summit of the genre. Since Beethoven's time, the string quartet has been an obligatory part of the composer's repertoire, and one of the highest peaks was undoubtedly reached by Schubert. Nevertheless, it is in Bartók's quartets that one finds the most profound, but also the most assimilated influence of Beethoven's quartets; one can speak of a "Haydn-Beethoven-Bartók" lineage - three composers sharing in many ways the same conception of form, of the motif and of its use, and especially in this particular genre.

Sonatas for violin

Besides the quartets, Beethoven wrote beautiful sonatas for violin and piano, the first ones being a direct inheritance from Mozart, while the last ones, notably the *"Kreutzer" Sonata,* depart from it to be pure Beethoven, this last sonata being almost a concerto for piano and violin. The last sonata (n° 10) is more introspective than the previous ones, prefiguring in this respect the last string quartets.

Sonatas for cello

Less well known than his violin sonatas or his quartets, his five *sonatas for cello and piano are* among Beethoven's truly innovative works. He develops very personal forms, far from the classical scheme that persists in his violin sonatas. With virtuosos such as Luigi Boccherini or Jean-Baptiste Bréval, the cello acquired notoriety as a solo instrument at the end of the XVIIIe century. However, after the *concertos* of Vivaldi and the importance of the cello in Mozart's chamber music, it is with Beethoven that the cello is treated for the first time in the genre of the classical sonata.

The first two sonatas (op. 5 n° 1 and op. 5 n° 2) were composed in 1796 and dedicated to King Frederick William II of Prussia. These are early works (Beethoven was 26 years old), which nevertheless present a certain fantasy and freedom of writing. Both have the same construction, namely a large introduction as a slow movement, followed by two fast movements of different tempo. These sonatas are thus far from the classical model, of which a perfect example can be found in the *piano sonatas opus 2*. The first of these sonatas, in *F* major, actually has a sonata form within it. Indeed, after the introduction, there is a section with this form: an *allegro*, an *adagio*, a *presto* and a return to the *allegro*. The final rondo has a ternary meter, contrasting with the binary of the previous movement. The second sonata, in *G* minor, has a completely different character. The development and contrapuntal passages are much more present. In the final *rondo*, a polyphony distributing a different role to the two soloists takes the place of imitation and the equal distribution of themes between the two instruments as it was practiced at the time, notably in Mozart's *violin sonatas.*

Beethoven did not compose another sonata until much later, in 1807. It is the sonata in A major op. 69, composed at the same period as the *symphonies n° 5 and 6*, the *Razoumovski quartets* and the *piano concerto n° 4*. The cello begins the first movement alone, during which we discover a theme that will be used again in the *arioso dolente* of the *piano sonata opus 110*. The second movement is a *scherzo* with a very marked syncopated rhythm, reminiscent of the corresponding movement of the *symphony n° 7*. This is followed by a very short slow movement, serving as an introduction to the *finale* as in the *"Aurore" sonata*, which has a tempo appropriate to a concluding movement.

Beethoven completed his journey in the cello sonatas in 1815, with the *two sonatas opus 102*. The *Allgemaine Musikalische Zeitung* said: "These two sonatas are certainly the most unusual and singular of what has been written for a long time, not only in this genre, but for the piano in general. Everything is different, completely different from what one is used to hearing, even from the master himself. This statement sounds like an echo when one knows that the manuscript of the *sonata in C major opus 102 n° 1* bears the title "free sonata for piano and cello". This work has indeed a strange construction: an *andante* leads without interruption to a *vivace* in *A* minor in sonata form whose theme is somewhat related to that of the *andante*. An *adagio* leads to a varied reprise of the *andante* and then to the *allegro vivace* finale, also in sonata form, whose development and coda reveal fugal writing, a first for Beethoven in sonata form. The second sonata of the group, in *D* major, is equally free. The second movement, an *adagio, is* the only large slow movement of the five cello sonatas. The work concludes with a four-part fugue, the last part of which has a harshness of harmony characteristic of Beethoven's fugues.

The freedom with which Beethoven breaks away from traditional melodic and harmonic formulas is evident in these sonatas.

Piano Trios

During his early years in Vienna, Beethoven already had a formidable reputation as a pianist. His first published composition, however, was not a work for solo piano, but a collection of three trios for piano, violin and cello composed between 1793 and 1795 and published in October 1795. These three trios, n° 1 in E flat major op. 1 n° 1, n° 2 in G major op. 1 n° 2, n° 3 in C minor op. 1 n° 3, were dedicated to Prince Karl von Lichnowsky, one of the composer's first patrons in Vienna.

Already in this first publication, Beethoven distinguishes himself from his illustrious predecessors in this musical form, such as Joseph Haydn and Mozart, whose trios only have three movements. Beethoven decided to place the three instruments on an equal footing, while he gave a more symphonic form to the structure of the work by adding a fourth movement. He also did not hesitate to delve into the writing, in order to create music that was truly complex and demanding, rather than a kind of salon entertainment.

The Trio No. 4 in B flat major, Op. 11, nicknamed "Gassenhauer" is a trio for piano, clarinet and cello in which the clarinet can be replaced by a violin. It was composed in 1797 and published in 1798, and dedicated to Countess Maria Whilhelmine von Thun, Beethoven's patron in Vienna. The trio has three movements. The theme of the variations in the last movement comes from a popular aria from the opera *L'amor marinaro* by Joseph Weigl.

Beethoven began composing the two Trios for Piano and Strings, Op. 70 in August 1808, just after completing the Sixth Symphony; perhaps the prominent role given to the cello is related to the composition, shortly before, of the Cello Sonata, Op. 69.

The Trio no.° 5 op. 70 no.° 1 in D major has three movements; its common name "The Spirits" (*Geister-Trio* in German) certainly comes from the mysterious opening Largo, full of ominous tremolos and trills. Appropriately, one of the movement's musical ideas comes from sketches for the witches' scene in an opera *Macbeth* that never saw the light of day.

The Trio n° 6 op. 70 n° 2, in E flat major, is in the same four-movement form; note the almost Schubertian lyricism of the third movement, an Allegretto in the minuet style. These two trios were dedicated to the Countess Maria von Erdödy, a close friend of the composer.

The last Piano Trio, Op. 97 in B-flat major, composed in 1811 and published in 1816, is known as "The Archduke," in honor of Beethoven's pupil and patron Archduke Rudolf, to whom it is dedicated. Unusually, the Scherzo and Trio precede the slow movement Andante cantabile, whose theme-and-variation structure follows the classical pattern of increasing difficulty and complexity of writing as the variations unfold. After a long coda, the discourse fades into silence until a cheerful motif leads the listener straight into the final rondo.

In addition to the seven large trios with opus numbers, Beethoven wrote two large sets of variations (Op. 44 and Op. 121a), two other trios published after his death (WoO

38 and WoO 39), and an Allegretto in *E-flat* Hess 48 for the same ensemble.

String Trios

The string trios were composed between 1792 and 1798. They preceded the generation of quartets and constitute the first works of Beethoven for solo strings. The genre of the trio is derived from the baroque trio sonata, where the bass, consisting here of a harpsichord and a cello, will see the harpsichord disappear with the independence taken by the cello, which until now only reinforced the harmonics of the latter.

Opus 3 was composed before 1794 and published in 1796. It is a trio in six movements in E flat major. It remains close to the spirit of entertainment. The three strings are treated here in a complementary way with a homogeneous distribution of the melodic roles. The Serenade in D major opus 8 dates from 1796-1797. This five-movement work is symmetrically constructed around a central adagio framed by two lyrical slow movements, all introduced and concluded by the same march. Finally, the trios opus 9 n° 1, n° 2 and n° 3 see their composition going back to 1797 and their publication taking place in July 1798. This opus is dedicated to Count von Browne, an officer in the Tsar's army. These trios are built in four movements according to the classical model of the quartet and the symphony. In the first (in *G* major) and third (in *C* minor), the scherzo replaces the minuet, while the second (in *D* major) remains perfectly classical.

Unlike most chamber music compositions, it is not known for which performers these trios were written. After Schubert, the string trio was practically abandoned.

Miscellaneous set

Although he wrote sonatas for piano and violin, piano and cello, quintets and string quartets, Beethoven also composed for less conventional ensembles. There are even some ensembles for which he composed only once. The majority of his works were composed during his younger years, a period when Beethoven was still searching for his own style. This did not prevent him from trying new formations later in life, such as variations for piano and flute around 1819. The piano remains Beethoven's preferred instrument, and this is reflected in his chamber music output, where a piano is almost always present.

In chronological order are the three quartets for piano, violin, viola and cello WoO 36 in 1785, the trio for piano, flute and bassoon WoO 37 in 1786, the sextet for two horns, two violins, viola and cello op. 81b in 1795, the quintet for piano, oboe, clarinet, horn and bassoon op. 16 in 1796, four pieces for mandolin and piano WoO 43/44 in 1796, the trio for piano, clarinet and cello op. 11 between

1797 and 1798, the septet for violin, viola, clarinet, horn, bassoon, cello and double bass op. 20 in 1799, the sonata for piano and horn op. 17 in 1800, the serenade for flute, violin and viola op. 25 in 1801, the quintet for two violins, two violas and cello op. 29 in 1801 and the themes and variations for piano and flute op. 105 and 107 from 1818 to 1820.

Sacred music

Beethoven composed an oratorio: *Christ on the Mount of Olives* (1801) for soloists, choir and orchestra op. 85, and two masses: the *Mass in C major*, op. 86 (1807), and especially the *Missa solemnis in D major*, op. 123 (1818-1822), one of the most important works of religious vocal music ever created.

Secular music

Finally, he is the author of several *song* cycles - including the one entitled "*To the Beloved Far Away*" - which, although they do not reach the depth of those of Franz Schubert (whom he discovered shortly before his death), are nonetheless of great quality.

List of main works

Symphonic music

- **Symphonies**
    - 1800 : *nº 1 in C major*, op. 21
    - 1802 : *nº 2 in D major*, op. 36
    - 1804 : *nº 3 in E flat major* " Eroica ", op. 55
    - 1806 : *nº 4 in B flat major*, op. 60
    - 1808 : *nº 5 in C minor*, op. 67
    - 1808 : *nº 6 in F major* " Pastorale ", op. 68
    - 1812 : *nº 7 in A major*, op. 92
    - 1813 : *nº 8 in F major*, op. 93
    - 1824 : *nº 9 in D minor*, op. 125
- **Openings**
    - 1801 : *The Creatures of Prometheus*, op. 43
    - 1805 : *Leonore I*, op. 138
    - 1805 : *Leonore II*, op. 72a
    - 1806 : *Leonore III*, op. 72a
    - 1807 : *Coriolan*, op. 62
    - 1810 : *Egmont*, op. 84
    - 1811 : *The Ruins of Athens*, op. 113
    - 1811 : *Le Roi Étienne*, op. 117
    - 1814 : *Fidelio*, op. 72b
    - 1815 : *Jour de fête*, op. 115

- ○ 1822 : *The Consecration of the House*, op. 124
- **Various works**
  - ○ 1808: *Choral Fantasy for piano, choir and orchestra*, Op. 80
  - ○ 1813 : *The Victory of Wellington*, op. 91

Concertos and concertante works

- **Concertos for piano**
  - ○ 1784 : *n° 0 in E flat major*, WoO 4
  - ○ 1798 : *n° 1 in C major*, op. 15
  - ○ 1795 : *n° 2 in B flat major*, op. 19
  - ○ 1802 : *n° 3 in C minor*, op. 37
  - ○ 1806 : *n° 4 in G major*, op. 58
  - ○ 1809 : *n° 5 in E flat major*, known as " l'Empereur ", op. 73

Beethoven also adapted a version for piano and orchestra of his own concerto for violin and orchestra in D major, Op. 61.

- **Other concertos**
  - ○ 1804: *Triple concerto for piano, violin and cello in C major*, op. 56
  - ○ 1806: *Violin Concerto in D major*, Op. 61
- **Concertante works**
  - ○ 1802 : *Romance for violin n° 1 in G major*, op. 40
  - ○ 1805 : *Romance for violin n° 2 in F major*, op. 50 composed in 1798

Music for piano

- **Sonatas for piano**
    - o 1783: *Three sonatas known as "à l'Électeur"*, WoO 47
    - o 1795 : *n° 1 in F minor*, op. 2 n° 1
    - o 1795 : *n° 2 in A major*, op. 2 n° 2
    - o 1795 : *n° 3 in C major*, op. 2 n° 3
    - o 1797 : *n° 4 in E flat major*, op. 7 *Grand Sonata for Harpsichord or Piano-Forte*
    - o 1798 : *n° 5 in C minor*, op. 10 n° 1 *for the Harpsichord or Piano-Forte*
    - o 1798 : *n° 6 in F major*, op. 10 n° 2 *for the Harpsichord or Piano-Forte*
    - o 1798 : *n° 7 in D major*, op. 10 n° 3 *for the Harpsichord or Piano-Forte*
    - o 1799 : *n° 8 in C minor* " Pathétique ", op. 13 *Grande Sonate pathétique pour le Clavecin ou Piano-Forte*
    - o 1799 : *n° 9 in E major*, op. 14 n° 1
    - o 1799 : *n° 10 in G major*, op. 14 n° 2
    - o 1800 : *n° 11 in B flat major*, op. 22
    - o 1801 : *n° 12 in A flat major*, op. 26 *Grande Sonate pour le Clavecin ou Forte-Piano*
    - o 1801: *n° 13 in E flat major* "Quasi una fantasia", op. 27 n° 1 *Sonata quasi una Fantasia per il Clavicembalo o Piano-Forte*

- 1801: *n° 14 in C sharp minor* "Quasi una fantasia" or "Moonlight", op. 27 n° 2 *Sonata quasi una Fantasia per il Clavicembalo o Piano-Forte*
- 1801 : *n° 15 in D major* " Pastorale ", op. 28
- 1802 : *n° 16 in G major*, op. 31 n° 1
- 1802 : *n° 17, in D minor* " the Storm ", op. 31 n° 2
- 1802 : *n° 18 in E flat major* known as "The Hunt", op. 31 n° 3
- 1798 : *n° 19 in G minor*, op. 49 n° 1
- 1796 : *n° 20 in G major*, op. 49 n° 2
- 1803 : *n° 21 in C major* " Waldstein ", op. 53
- 1804 : *n° 22 in F major*, op. 54
- 1805 : *n° 23 in F minor* " Appassionata ", op. 57
- 1809 : *n° 24 in F sharp major* " à Thérèse ", op. 78
- 1808 : *n° 25 in G major* " le Coucou ", op. 79
- 1810 : *n° 26, in E flat major* " les Adieux ", op. 81a
- 1814 : *n° 27 in E minor*, op. 90
- 1816 : *n° 28 in A major*, op. 101

- 1818 : *n° 29 in B flat major* " Hammerklavier ", op. 106
- 1820 : *n° 30 in E major*, op. 109
- 1821 : *n° 31 in A flat major*, op. 110
- 1822 : *n° 32 in C minor*, op. 111
- **Variations for piano**
  - 1802 : *Six variations in F major*, op. 34
  - 1802 : *Fifteen heroic variations in E flat major*, op. 35
  - 1802: *Six variations in G major on "Nel cor più non mi sento"*, WoO 70
  - 1803: *Seven variations in C major on "God save the King"*, WoO 78
  - 1803: *Five variations in D major on "Rule Britannia"*, WoO 79
  - 1806: *Thirty-two variations in C minor on an original theme*, WoO 80
  - 1823 : *Thirty-three variations in C major on a waltz by Diabelli*, op. 120
- **Bagatelles for piano**
  - 1802 : *Seven bagatelles*, op. 33
  - 1810: *Bagatelle in A minor "for Elise"*, WoO 59
  - 1818 : *Bagatelle in B flat major*, WoO 60
  - 1822 : *Eleven bagatelles*, op. 119
  - 1824 : *Six bagatelles*, op. 126
- **Fantasy for piano**

- 1809 : *Fantasia for piano in G minor*, op. 77

Chamber music

- **String quartets**
  - 1801 : *n° 1 in F major*, op. 18 n° 1 composed in 1799
  - 1801 : *n° 2 in G major*, op. 18 n° 2 composed in 1799
  - 1801 : *n° 3 in D major*, op. 18 n° 3 composed in 1798
  - 1801 : *n° 4 in C minor*, op. 18 n° 4 composed in 1799
  - 1801 : *n° 5 in A major*, op. 18 n° 5 composed in 1799
  - 1801 : *n° 6 in B flat major*, op. 18 n° 6 composed in 1799
  - 1806 : *n° 7 in F major* " Razumovsky ", op. 59 n° 1
  - 1806 : *n° 8 in E minor* " Razumovsky ", op. 59 n° 2
  - 1806 : *n° 9 in C major* " Razumovsky ", op. 59 n° 3
  - 1809 : *n° 10 in E flat major* " les Harpes ", op. 74
  - 1810 : *n° 11 in F minor* " Serioso ", op. 95
  - 1824 : *n° 12 in E flat major*, op. 127
  - 1825 : *n° 13 in B flat major*, op. 130

- 1826 : *n° 14 in C sharp minor*, op. 131
- 1825 : *n° 15 in A minor*, op. 132
- 1826 : *n° 16 in F major*, op. 135
- 1825 : *Great Fugue in B flat major*, op. 133

- **Sonatas for violin and piano**
  - 1798 : *n° 1 in D major*, op. 12 n° 1
  - 1798 : *n° 2 in A major*, op. 12 n° 2
  - 1798 : *n° 3 in E flat major*, op. 12 n° 3
  - 1801 : *n° 4 in A minor*, op. 23
  - 1801 : *n° 5 in F major* " le Printemps ", op. 24
  - 1802 : *n° 6 in A major*, op. 30 n° 1
  - 1802 : *n° 7 in C minor*, op. 30 n° 2
  - 1802 : *n° 8 in G major*, op. 30 n° 3
  - 1803 : *n° 9 in A major* " à Kreutzer ", op. 47
  - 1812 : *n° 10 in G major*, op. 96

- **Sonatas for cello and piano**
  - 1796 : *n° 1 in F major*, op. 5 n° 1
  - 1796 : *n° 2 in G minor*, op. 5 n° 2
  - 1808 : *n° 3 in A major*, op. 69
  - 1815 : *n° 4 in C major*, op. 102 n° 1
  - 1815 : *n° 5 in D major*, op. 102 n° 2

- **Trios for piano, violin and cello**
  - 1794 : *n° 1 in E flat major*, op. 1 n° 1
  - 1794 : *n° 2 in G major*, op. 1 n° 2

- o 1794 : *n° 3 in C minor*, op. 1 n° 3
- o 1798 : *n° 4 in B flat major*, op. 11
- o 1808: *n° 5 in D major*, known as "The Spirits", op. 70 n° 1
- o 1808 : *n° 6 in E flat major*, op. 70 n° 2
- o 1811 : *n° 7 in B flat major* " à l'Archiduc ", op. 97
- **Various works**
  - o 1792 : *Wind octet in E flat major*, op. 103
  - o 1792 : *String Trio n° 1 in E flat major*, op. 3
  - o 1796 : *String Trio n° 2 in D major*, op. 8
  - o 1798 : *String Trio n° 3 in G major*, op. 9 n° 1
  - o 1798: *String Trio n° 4 in D major*, op. 9 n° 2
  - o 1798: *String Trio n° 5 in C minor*, op. 9 n° 3
  - o 1796 : *String Quintet n° 1 in E flat major*, op. 4
  - o 1801 : *String Quintet n° 2 in C major*, op. 29
  - o 1817 : *String Quintet n° 3 in C minor*, op. 104
  - o 1800 : *Sonata for horn and piano in F major*, op. 17

- o 1800: *Septet for strings and winds in E flat major*, op. 20

Vocal music
- **Opera**
  - o 1814 : *Fidelio*, op. 72 composed in 1805
- **Sacred music**
  - o 1801 : *Christ on the Mount of Olives*, oratorio, op. 85
  - o 1807 : *Mass in C major*, op. 86
  - o 1827 : *Missa solemnis in D major*, op. 123 composed in 1818
- **Cantata**
  - o 1790 : *Funeral cantata on the death of Emperor Joseph II*, for soloists, choir and orchestra WoO87
  - o 1790 : *Cantata on the accession of Emperor Leopold II*, for soloists, choir and orchestra WoO88
  - o 1814: *Der glorreiche Augenblick*, cantata for soloists, choir and orchestra, Op. 136
  - o 1815: *Meeresstille und glückliche Fahrt*, cantata for choir and orchestra, op. 112
  - o 1822: *Opferlied ("Die Flamme lodert")*, for soprano, choir and orchestra, op. 121b
- **Melodies**
  - o 1796 : *Adelaide*, cantata for one voice, op. 46

- 1796: *Ah! Perfido*, scene and aria op. 65 for soprano and orchestra on a text by Metastasio
- 1803: *Six lieder on poems by Christian Fürchtegott Gellert*, op. 48
- 1809 : *Six lieder on poems by Goethe*, op. 75
- 1810 : *Three lieder on poems by Goethe*, op. 83
- 1813 : *À l'espérance*, lied, op. 94
- 1816: *To the Distant Beloved*, cycle of six lieder, Op. 98

Contemporary use

Today, his work is featured in numerous films, radio show credits and commercials. These include:

- 1971: In Stanley Kubrick's *Clockwork Orange*, Alex De Large listens to the second movement of 9e symphony as well as the *Ode to Joy*;

- 1985: the anthem of the European Union is taken from the Symphony n° 9;

Beethoven's life has also inspired several films, including:

- 1909: *Beethoven* by Victorin Jasset with Harry Baur ;

- 1936: *Un grand amour de Beethoven* by Abel Gance with Harry Baur ;

- 1942: *Loved by the Gods* by Karl Hartl with René Deltgen ;

- 1949: *Eroïca* by Walter Kolm-Veltée with Ewald Balser as Beethoven ;

- 1994: *Ludwig van B.* by Bernard Rose with Gary Oldman as Beethoven ;

- 2005: *Copying Beethoven* by Agnieszka Holland features the composer played by Ed Harris in love with his assistant, Anna Holtz, played by Diane Kruger ;

- 2020 : Louis van Beethoven is a biographical film that came in commemoration of the 250^e anniversary of Beethoven's birth.

Recordings made with instruments from Beethoven's time

- Malcolm Bilson, Tom Beghin, David Breitman, Ursula Dütschler, Zvi Meniker, Bart van Oort, Andrew Willis. Ludwig van Beethoven. *The complete Piano Sonatas on Period Instruments*

- András Schiff. Ludwig van Beethoven. *Beethoven's Broadwood Piano*

- Robert Levin, John Eliot Gardiner. Ludwig van Beethoven. *Piano Concertos.* Walter (Paul McNulty)

- Ronald Brautigam. Ludwig van Beethoven. *Complete Works for Solo Piano.* Walter, Stein, Graf (Paul McNulty)

Filmography

- 1909: *Beethoven* by Victorin Jasset with Harry Baur ;

- 1912: *The Glory and Sorrow of Ludwig Van Beethoven* by Georges André Lacroix with Ewald Balser ;

- 1918: *Martyr of His Heart* by Emil Justitz with Fritz Kortner ;

- 1926: *Franz Schuberts letzte Liebe* by Alfred Deutsch-German with Theodor Weiser ;

- 1927 :

  - *The Wild Hunt of Lützow. The heroic fate of Theodor Körner and his last love* by Richard Oswald with Albert Steinrück,

  - *Beethoven* (*Das Leben des Beethoven*) by Hans Otto with Fritz Kortner ;

- 1936: *Un grand amour de Beethoven* by Abel Gance with Harry Baur ;

- 1940 : *Serenade* by Jean Boyer with Auguste Boverio ;

- 1941: *The Great Awakening* by Reinhold Schünzel with Alan Curtis ;

- 1942 :

- $\circ$ *Rossini* by Mario Bonnard with Memo Benassi,

- $\circ$ *Loved by the gods* by Karl Hartl with René Deltgen ;

- 1943: *Heavenly Music* by Josef Berne with Steven Geray ;

- 1948: *The Mozart Story* by Karl Hartl and Frank Wisbar with René Deltgen ;

- 1949: *Eroïca* by Walter Kolm-Veltée with Ewald Balser ;

- 1955 : *Napoleon* by Sacha Guitry with Erich von Stroheim ;

- 1958: *The House of the Three Girls* by Ernst Marischka with Ewald Balser ;

- 1962: *The Magnificent Rebel* by Georg Tressler with Carl Boehm ;

- 1969: *Ludwig van* by Mauricio Kagel, Beethoven is mentioned;

- 1976: *Beethoven - Days in a Life* by Horst Seemann with Donatas Banionis ;

- 1977: *I cuaderni di conversazione di Ludwig van Beethoven* by Silverio Blasi with Maurice Mariaud ;

- 1985: *Beethoven's Nephew* by Paul Morrissey with Wolfgang Reichmann ;

- 1989 : *The Excellent Adventure of Bill* by Stephen Herek with Clifford David ;

- 1991 :

  - *Rossini!* by Mario Monicelli with Vittorio Gassman,

  - *Not Mozart: Letters, Riddles and Writs* by Jeremy Newson with Tony Rohr ;

- 1992: *Beethoven Lives Upstairs* by David Devine with Neil Munro ;

- 1994: *Ludwig van B.* by Bernard Rose with Gary Oldman ;

- 2003: *Eroica* by Simon Cellan Jones with Ian Hart ;

- 2005: *Copying Beethoven* by Agnieszka Holland features the composer played by Ed Harris in love with his assistant, Anna Holtz, played by Diane Kruger.

- 2020 : *Louis van Beethoven* by Niki Stein with Colin Pütz (child), Anselm Bresgott (youth) and Tobias Moretti (adutle).

Exhibitions

- 2017 : "Ludwig van. The Beethoven Myth" at the Philharmonie de Paris, curated by Marie-Pauline Martin and Colin Lemoine.

- 2018: "Beethoven *Loves the* Brentanos," San Jose State University Beethoven Center.

Other books by United Library

https://campsite.bio/unitedlibrary

Ingram Content Group UK Ltd.
Milton Keynes UK
UKHW020708170423
420292UK00015B/793

9 789493 311855